The World's Best Catholic Jokes

John Gurney

The World's Best Catholic Jokes

Illustrations by Louis Silvestro

ANGUS
& ROBERTSON
PUBLISHERS

ANGUS & ROBERTSON PUBLISHERS

Unit 4, Eden Park, 31 Waterloo Road,
North Ryde, NSW, Australia 2113, and
16 Golden Square, London W1R 4BN,
United Kingdom

First published in Australia by
Angus & Robertson Publishers in 1986
First published in the United Kingdom by
Angus & Robertson (UK) Ltd in 1986

Copyright © John Gurney 1986

ISBN 0 207 15001 X

Typeset in 12pt Palatino by
New Faces, Bedford
Printed in the United Kingdom by
Hazell Watson & Viney Ltd

Introduction

For centuries the Catholic faith has been a source of mystery and misunderstanding to those outside it. This modest collection will in no way clear up that mystery and misunderstanding. Instead it will highlight some of the mystery and misunderstandings that exist on the *inside* of that great organisation.

Probably because of the number of Irish Catholics who already come in for some kidding, most Catholics take jokes about their church in good part. Indeed they come to expect it. It is therefore our hope that all readers, Catholics included, will enjoy this gentle leg-pull.

John Gurney

To escape from the worries of everyday life, William joined a religious order where all the members took a vow of silence. On only one day each year were the members allowed to speak, and then they could each say only two words.

After he had been in the order for a year, Brother William was brought to the Abbot's study.

"You are permitted to say two words only. Do you understand?"

Brother William nodded.

"Do you wish to speak?"

He nodded again.

"Then what are your two words?"

"More food."

Another year went by and again he was brought to the Abbot's study.

"Do you wish to speak?"

Nod.

"What are your two words?"

"More blankets."

The third year went by and he was brought to the Abbot again.

"Do you wish to speak?"

Nod.

"What are your two words?"

"I quit."

"It's a good thing too," said the Abbot. "You've done nothing but complain ever since you got here."

An attractive young woman was about to enter St Philomene's in a topless dress. She was intercepted by the new curate.

"I'm very sorry, but I can't let you go into church like that."

The young lady protested:

"But I have a divine right…"

"…and a divine left too, but you still can't come into the church like that."

These days many people have difficulty in understanding what a miracle is. One such person was Pat – even though his priest explained the subject with great clarity and patience. Pat was still not satisfied.

"Father, could you be giving me an example?"

The priest sighed. "All right, Pat. Turn around."

When he did so the reverend gentleman gave him a hearty boot in the backside.

"Now Pat, did you feel that?"

"I should say I did."

"Well, Pat, it would have been a miracle if you hadn't."

Father Gilligan was a priest who loved to collect stories which he used to illustrate his sermons and conversations. He had once told a colleague, Father Whelan, that his sister, who kept house for him, was critically ill. "I'm afeared there's very little hope for her. Such a shame. A wonderful woman, you know. She's nearly a saint."

Some months later, after the sister had died, the two priests met again.

"A great loss," Father Whelan consoled.

"Yes," said Father Gilligan. "It reminds me of the man who was persuaded to turn his dog into a greyhound. He was told to give it two potatoes the size of golf balls every day together with an ounce of salt. This was to be its only food.

"After a fortnight he was to cut back the dog's ration to one potato and an ounce of salt. Two weeks after that he was to cut back to half a potato a day with an ounce of salt. By that time it should be starting to look like a greyhound.

"Six weeks later he met his adviser who asked how he had got on with the diet. 'I tried it on the dog,' he said, 'and, you know, it nearly worked. The dog was nearly a greyhound when he died.' So it was with my sister. She was nearly a saint, but she died."

F ather Clancy rang up the local council to ask that a dead goat be removed from in front of his house. The clerk who took the call thought he'd be smart:

"I thought you priests took care of the dead," he said.

"We do," said Father Clancy. "But first we have to get in touch with their relatives."

F ather Conaghan had been curate in the parish for five years and now he was leaving to go to a parish of his own. The send-off celebration took the form of a huge barbecue to which most of the parish came.

During the afternoon one of the older ladies came gushing to Father Conaghan:

"I don't know how we'll ever do without you. Until you came we didn't know what sin was."

After many years Father Sullivan left his missionary parish to make a trip back to his native Ireland. In his travels through the Emerald Isle he spent a few days in a city noted for the number of different bells that ring at all times. Out walking one afternoon, he was so enchanted by the sound of these bells that he commented on them to a nearby roadworker.

"Aren't the bells lovely?" he said.

"What?"

"I said aren't all the bells lovely?"

"What did you say?"

"I SAID AREN'T ALL THE BELLS LOVELY?"

"I'm sorry. I can't hear what you're saying for the noise of those goddam bells."

An advertising salesman from a suburban newspaper called at Harris's Pharmacy at Caraway's Hill. Old Mr Harris was not impressed with his story.

"Been in business here for twenty-seven years and I've never had to advertise yet."

"Then perhaps you could tell me, what is that building on the hill?"

"That's St Philomene's church."

"Been there long?"

"More than eighty years."

"Well, they still ring the bell."

D anny went to Father Ignatius privately to seek his advice.

"Father, I'm a bit worried. I've done something I don't think I should have, and I want to know whether I'm likely to be thrown out of the Church."

"What sort of thing?"

"Well, it's like this. Maureen and I have only been married a few weeks, as you know. The other day I came up behind her as she was bending over getting something out of the freezer and – I don't know what came over me – I let her have it. Just like that. Bang. Will I be thrown out of the Church?"

"Well now, Danny, the Church does not actually condone behaviour of that sort, but at the same time you are in the married state, and so do enjoy certain rights and privileges. No. You won't be thrown out of the Church. What made you think you'd be thrown out of the Church anyway?"

"Well, we were thrown out of Safeway's."

On a warm Saturday afternoon the parish priest was reading his office in the confessional of his deserted church. He heard two pairs of children's footsteps enter the church, and then a lot of whispering. This gradually became louder until he could hear the voices of two small boys.

"You go first."

"No. You go first."

"I'll go after you go."

This continued until one of the boys came in and made his confession. After he went out, the priest heard him say to the other boy:

"It's all right. He can't do anything to you. They've got him locked up inside some kind of meat safe."

"Father, I spent an hour this morning just looking in the mirror and thinking how beautiful I was," a woman confessed to her priest. "Will I have to do penance?"

"No. You only do penance for a sin, not a mistake."

P addy was in the confessional. After the pre-liminary rituals the priest asked for specifics.

"What have you been up to, Paddy?"

"Pinchin' timber, Father."

"Three Hail Marys."

Next week Paddy was back again.

"What is it this time, Paddy?"

"Pinchin' timber again, Father."

"Three Hail Marys."

But the third week, when Paddy confessed he'd been pinching timber again, the priest paused for a time before he gave him his penance.

"Paddy, I'm going to ask you to make a novena for me."

"Sure now, Father. You get me the plans and I'll pinch the timber."

F ather O'Malley was at the races and was horrified to see and hear one of his parishioners roaring out the most frightful language during a race.

"Use the bloody whip on the bastard you dopey cow. How did a useless bastard like you get a bloody mount like this anyway?" It just went on and on.

After the race Father O'Malley took him aside.

"George, there's no need for all this. Take it quietly. Now when I've got a bet on I just say, 'Dear Lord, let him get away well from the barrier.' And later I just say, 'Lord, let my horse come up to a good position in the field.' And as they're coming round the turn I say, 'Lord, let him make a run down the outside and come home the winner.' It always works. George, there's no need of all this cursing and swearing. You try it."

In the next race George tried out the priest's advice. As promised, his horse got away well from the barrier. Later it took a good position in the field and as they were coming round the turn into the straight George murmured, "Thank you, Lord. I'll take it from here. USE THE BLOODY WHIP ON THE BASTARD YOU DOPEY COW..."

P addy was dying. The doctor had given him only a few hours to live. He sent for the priest.

"Ah, Paddy. Sorry and all it is I am to see you looking so poorly."

"Yes, Father. The doctor do be giving me just a few hours to live."

"Ay Paddy, and you've been sending for me so that you can make your peace with Almighty God and go to your Maker with a clear conscience."

"Well, no Father. That's not what I've been sending for you for at all. I wanted to see you so that I could be telling you that I've decided to renounce the Catholic faith and join the Masons."

"Ah Paddy, your mind must be wandering. We'll pay no heed to that."

"My mind's not wandering at all, Father. I've made up my mind in cold blood. I'm going to renounce the Catholic faith and join the Masons."

"But why, Paddy? In heaven's name why?"

"Well, Father, if somebody's got to die, isn't it better that it be one of them bastards than one of us?"

Saints in heaven are sometimes permitted to visit the earth in disguise. St Theresa had always wanted to go to Hollywood but Gabriel was in charge of the roster and wouldn't let her. He felt that the temptations of the movie capital would prove too much even for a saint. She finally convinced him that no harm would come to her, and headed down on the first earthbound cloud.

Weeks and months went by and there was no word from her, and at last Gabriel put through a call to Los Angeles.

The phone rang and a voice answered:

"Terry here. Who's speaking? Gabby – dahling! How perfectly marvellous to hear from you..."

A visiting priest came to a small country town and asked a young boy to direct him to the church where he was preaching that evening. After the boy had given him the directions, the priest said to him:

"You must come along tonight and bring all your friends."

"What for?"

"Because I'll tell you all how to get to heaven."

"You must be joking. You didn't even know how to get to the church."

"Which parable in the Bible do you like best, David?" Sister Louisa asked her youngest pupil in Religious Instruction.

"The one about the fellow that loafs and fishes."

The priest was sitting one afternoon in the sacristy of his church, just behind the statue of Mary, when one of the little girls from the parish primary school came into the church and approached the statue.

"Dear Our Lady. Can I bring my friend Cheryl to the parish picnic next month? She's not a Catholic."

The priest heard this.

"She can't come," he boomed.

At which the supplicant piped up:

"You keep quiet God. I'm talking to your Mother."

A country priest met a neighbour who never came to church, although he was over sixty years old. He reproached him with this.

"I suppose you couldn't even tell me who made you."

"No, as a matter of fact I couldn't."

A small boy came past at the same time and the priest turned to him.

"Who made you, child?"

"God, Father."

"There you are. Aren't you ashamed that a mere child of five or six years old can tell me who made him, while you that are so old can't?"

"Maybe so. But it's no wonder he can remember. He was only made the other day. But me – it's sixty years since I was made."

Sister Magdalene had spent the whole period of Religious Instruction telling her children about repentance. At the end she asked the class:

"What do we have to do first before we can obtain forgiveness of our sins?"

Young Michael O'Shea was the first to answer. "Sin."

"Nice to see you coming along to church again," said the parish priest to one of his parishioners. "Is it because of my sermons?"

"Not yours. My wife's."

Father Cassidy was preaching a sermon on the Ten Commandments. When he got to the Commandment 'Thou shalt not steal' he noticed a little man at the front shuffling in a very uneasy way. But later, when he dealt with the Commandment 'Thou shalt not commit adultery', the same man sighed and smiled.

Afterwards he remarked to the man on his behaviour and asked him if he would care to explain.

"Well, Father, while you were talking about 'Thou shalt not steal' I noticed that my umbrella was missing. But as soon as you got to 'Thou shalt not commit adultery', I knew straightaway what I'd done with it."

F ather Moloney was getting very worked up in his sermon on repentance.

"If a man is caught stealing he should be buried with his hand uncovered. And if a man is convicted of telling lies he should be buried with his tongue sticking out of the ground. And if a man is guilty of adultery..."

"Just a minute, Father," interrupted one of the congregation. "If you're going to say what I think you're going to say, this whole damned town will look like an asparagus patch."

"What's your new parish priest like, Terry?"
"A good enough fellow except for his sermons. After you've been listening to him for two hours, you look at your watch and it's only been twenty minutes."

One Sunday Father Murray announced that the following week his sermon would be on the topic of lying. He asked that through the week everyone should read the 51st Chapter of Genesis.

The following week he asked for a show of hands of all those who had not read the 51st Chapter of Genesis. Not one hand was raised.

"Thank you. My sermon on the subject of lying should be most appropriate. There is no 51st Chapter of Genesis."

F ather O'Reilly was explaining faith to his congregation.

"In the front row we have Sean and Maureen O'Malley with their five children. Maureen knows they are her children. That's knowledge. Sean believes they are his children. That's faith."

"F aith," wrote the seminarian in his exam paper, "is the faculty by which we are enabled to believe that which we know is not true."

After his first appearance in the pulpit, the new curate asked Father Cassidy what he'd thought of his performance.

"Did I put enough fire into my sermon?"

"Yes you did to be sure. But from the reaction I'd say it might have been better to have put a lot of the sermon into the fire."

Father Flannagan was shaking hands with members of his flock after mass. He was rather pleased when one of them told him that his sermon had been like the peace and mercy of God.

Thinking about it afterwards, however, he was not so sure. He remembered the quotation, "The peace of God passeth all understanding and His mercy endureth forever."

A man went to his doctor with a weight problem.

"I want to lose weight, but it's no good putting me on a diet. I've had them before and they never did me any good."

"The only thing I can suggest is a rather unusual Indian remedy using exercise only. There's no dieting. You can eat what you like. What you have to do is have violent, passionate sexual intercourse at least four times a night. You understand? Come back and see me in a month."

At the end of one month the doctor saw his patient again.

"How much weight have you lost?"

"Only about half a pound."

"How many times have you had sexual intercourse in the last month?"

"Eleven times."

"Good heavens man, that's not nearly enough."

"Perhaps not, but it's pretty good for a country priest with a small parish."

At the graduation ceremony of St Angela's Girls' College, Sister Theresa was addressing the girls about their future.

"Today is a big step into your future life. You will meet with many temptations, and I urge you to remember the teachings and ideals you have learned here at St Angela's. You will undoubtedly meet many men who will try to take advantage of you sexually. Do not respond to their advances. Remember, one hour of pleasure can result in the ruin of your whole life, and that of your family. Do any of you have any questions?"

"Yes, Sister. How do you make it last an hour?"

"Do you know, Father, the mother has eleven children!" The curate was telling Father Cassidy about a new family that had moved into the parish.

"Ah, it's good to see an old-fashioned Catholic family raising so many sons and daughters for the Church."

"But they're not Catholics, Father. They're Methodists."

"How disgusting! Sex mad. Absolutely no self control."

A London prostitute was telling her girl friend about her new enthusiasm for the Catholic Church.

"You know that cold, wet night we had last week? Well, to get out of the rain I went into Westminster Cathedral. When I got inside there's this line of people so I got in the line with all the others. After a while I found myself in this little booth and there's a priest on the other side of this window. He says to me, 'What have you been doing?' So I told him. Then he told me that I should do the stations.

"Do you know that since then I've done Waterloo, Kings Cross, Marylebone and Paddington, and I'm making a bundle."

A t the convent school reunion the Reverend Mother was asking each of her ex-pupils what career she had chosen.

"I've become a prostitute," said one, and the Reverend Mother promptly fainted.

When she was revived she asked the girl what she had said.

"A prostitute," repeated the girl.

"Thank heavens," said the Reverend Mother, "I thought for a moment you had said a Protestant."

Peter was a Catholic and Charles, his next door neighbour, was a Presbyterian. They were good friends, and on summer evenings enjoyed watering their vegetable gardens and yarning over the fence.

One night, as Charles was watering a prolific crop of sprouts, he was reminded of a question he'd been meaning to ask his neighbour.

"Tell me something, Peter. You Catholics aren't supposed to use any form of birth control, while we can use anything at all. And yet you've only got two kids, and we've got five. How do you account for that?"

"Simple," his friend replied. "We use the safe period."

"Safe period? Never heard of it. What's the safe period?"

"Every second Thursday when you go to Lodge."

A Catholic priest and a Protestant minister had a long argument about their respective beliefs. At last they agreed to differ. In parting, the priest said, "You worship God your way, and I'll worship Him His way."

A young Irish police officer waved a car down for going through a red light. All ready to read the riot act to the driver, he came up to the vehicle to find it being driven by a Catholic priest.

"Father, you've just driven through a red light I'm afraid. I won't say anything about it except to warn you to be specially careful at the next set of lights."

"A particularly dangerous intersection, is it?" enquired the priest.

"Yes, Father. The cop on duty there is a Baptist."

The new curate's first official duty was to preside at the Women's Bible Class, but instead of discussing religious matters the women spent the whole time chattering about their aches and pains, their children's tonsils and appendixes, and their husbands' back troubles and bad hearts.

When the curate returned to the presbytery, Father Cassidy asked him how he had got on.

"Well," said the younger man, "it wasn't so much a Bible Class as an Organ Recital."

After mass a woman asked her husband what he thought of the mink stole on the lady who had been sitting in front of him.

"I didn't notice. I must have dozed off."

"I must say! A lot of good coming to mass does you."

Young Michael Mahoney was attending mass for the first time, and he couldn't take his eyes off the choir-boys, all in their white surplices. At last he whispered to his father:

"Daddy, are they all going to have their hair cut?"

During mass the young boy was very restless and his dad had a lot of trouble keeping him still. The lad was intrigued by the red sanctuary lamp and, after a time, he clutched his father's arm.

"Dad! Dad! When it turns green can we go?"

Behind the inn at Bethlehem the shepherds found the stable where the new-born child who was to be the hope of Israel lay. They opened the creaking door and saw in the lamplight for the first time the holy family. Joseph called softly to them.

"Come inside."

The floor was covered with straw and none of the men saw the rake that was lying in it with its prongs upward. One of them stepped on it and the handle flew up and dealt him a cruel blow on the forehead.

"Jesus Christ!" he exclaimed.

"Now that's a good idea," said Joseph. "We were thinking of calling Him Fred."

The parish council of St Michael's were simple people and their parish priest was a bit simple too. When it came to their notice that the poor box had been robbed twice in the last month, they passed a resolution that the box be moved to a position high above the floor where robbers could not reach it.

When it was pointed out that donors wishing to put money in the box would not be able to reach it either, the parish council passed another resolution that a flight of steps be constructed to enable donors to leave their donations in the poor box.

The sister at St Luke's Hospital was taking the particulars of the patients. One man gave his name and age but was reluctant to admit to having any next of kin.

"Surely you must have someone – a relative we can contact."

"Only my sister, but she'd be no good. She's only a nun."

"Only a nun? I'll have you know that she's married to the Son of God."

"Is that so? Well in that case, send the bill to my brother-in-law."

Which calls to mind the story about two elderly Jewish gentlemen who sought refuge from the cold wet weather inside St Patrick's cathedral. A ceremony was being conducted at the high altar in which sixty young women who had been novices in a religious order were being inducted as sisters.

A young priest saw the two unusual visitors in the body of the church and approached them.

"Is there anything I can do to help you?"

"It's perfectly all right, thank you. We're from the groom's side."

"Why were you so long over at the presbytery?" the Mother Superior asked a young novice.

"Father was showing me how to blow the Horn of Plenty."

"The old rogue. He told me it was the Trumpet of Gabriel."

Sister Theresa was the winner of the huge final jackpot at the church bingo party. She decided to fulfil a secret wish she had had for many years. She bought herself a full-length fur coat. The day she unpacked it she wore it down the street, to the envy of all the women she met.

Suddenly her Bishop drew up to the kerb in his official limousine. He rebuked her for not putting her windfall to better use.

"I remind you, Sister, that no saint has ever been known to require an expensive fur coat."

"True, but then, can you tell me one character in the Bible who rolled round the Holy Land in a Mercedes Benz?"

T wo nuns were walking to church together when they passed their Mother Superior.

"Good morning, Mother," they both said.

"Good morning, Sisters," grunted the Mother Superior angrily.

One of the sisters murmured to the other:

"Looks as though she got out of the wrong side of the bed."

Mother spun round.

"What was that you said, Sister?" she demanded.

"I just said, 'It looks as though you got out of the wrong side of the bed'. You've got Father's slippers on."

H ow about the fellow who stopped his dry cleaning van in the driveway of the convent and touted for trade.

"Hey in there," he yelled. "Have you got any dirty habits?"

"You seem to have very small congregations in your church," remarked one girl to another.

"We do indeed. Sometimes the congregation is so small that when the priest says 'dearly beloved' it's as if he's proposing to you."

"I felt so sorry for your wife this morning in church when she had that terrific attack of coughing. Everyone was staring at her."

"That was the whole idea. She was wearing her new spring hat."

O ne of the oldest jokes in the history of the Catholic Church is told of Saint Francis. One day this good man was working in the vegetable garden of the monastery when another monk came to him, all agog.

"Do you know there is a monk in a city forty miles away who has made a machine that can think?" he said excitedly.

St Francis was unmoved.

"When you find a machine that has made a monk that can think, let me know."

T he cyclone swept in from the Timor Sea and dumped millions of tons of water on the little town of St Lawrence, usually a dry part of tropical Australia. The country had been without rain for many months, but now the floodwaters were rising rapidly. Terry and Mike climbed onto the roof of the barn and hoped it would be high enough to keep them safe. After a time Terry spoke.

"Mike, do you remember last Sunday in mass when Father Halloran said a special prayer for rain?"

"Yes Terry, I do."

"Well, when you come to think of it, this is a pretty good effort for a little church like ours."

F red was a funny little character. He never seemed to do any work, always had plenty of money, and claimed to be on first name terms with famous people all over the world – film stars, heads of state – he knew them all. Tom was not convinced. One day he said to Fred:

"All this stuff you go on with about being close friends with so many famous people, I think it's all talk. In my opinion you're just one big bullshit merchant."

Fred shrugged.

"Can you take a few days off? I'll take you on a little trip and prove to you that I'm not bluffing. I'll be glad of an excuse to travel."

They booked air tickets and the next day they flew out. Their first stop was Washington DC. Without any appointment Fred took them to the White House and asked to see the president. Mr Reagan came out all smiles, wrung Fred's hand, and said, "Great to see you again, Fred."

After a short stay they headed for Europe. En route they overnighted in New York. While they were having dinner in a fine restaurant, who should walk in but Frank Sinatra. When he saw them he headed straight for their table and pumped Fred's hand: "Good to see you again, Fred. How long can you stay?"

Next stop was Rome. Fred took Tom to St Peter's Square. It was crowded with people. He said to Tom, "Keep your eye on that balcony up there. I'm going to leave you here for a while."

After a short wait there came a cheer from the crowd. Two figures had appeared on the balcony. One of them was His Holiness the Pope in all his

regalia, the other was Fred. They had their arms around each other. Tom was flabbergasted. He was even more so when the man standing next to him nudged him in the ribs and said:

"Who's the fellow up on the balcony with Fred?"

Two missionary sisters were walking through the jungle when suddenly they were attacked by two wild men and raped. After their attackers had gone they were straightening themselves up when one said:

"What bad luck! To be raped twice in the same day."

"What do you mean, twice?"

"Well, we have to come back this way, don't we?"

When Bishop Fulton Sheen made the first of many appearances on television, he stopped for a cup of coffee in the canteen attached to the studio. He was in full robes, with his red cape already in place. The girl behind the counter was used to actors in all sorts of costume and took it all in her stride:

"What's yours, Cock Robin?"

Two boys at school together were forever trading insults. After they left, one went into the Army, the other went into the Church. They did well and one was promoted to Colonel while the other became a Bishop.

One day they met on a railway platform, each wearing full regalia. The Bishop opened the conversation.

"Excuse me, porter. Am I on the right platform for Liverpool?"

"Yes, madam, you are, but do you think you should be travelling in your condition?"

When little Cathy went to mass for the first time she was fascinated. She peered around in all directions and then tugged her father's sleeve.

"Where's God, Daddy?"

Her father pointed towards the altar. Just then the sanctus bells rang. Another tug.

"Shouldn't He answer His phone?"

One thing Father O'Leary enjoyed more than anything else was going to the fights on Friday night. Every week he could be seen in the inner ringside cheering and urging. One week he took along his friend Len Anderson, who was not himself a Catholic and who didn't know very much about boxing.

"Don't be worrying, Len. I'll be after explaining it all to you."

They took their places and Father O'Leary showed Len which was the red corner and which the blue. He pointed up to the booth where the press and radio commentators sat. The man in white, he revealed, was the referee.

Then the first of the fighters came in. As he stepped through the ropes he wiped his feet in a tray.

"That's full of resin so he won't slip on the canvas during the fight."

When both contestants were in the ring they sat in their corners while their trainers talked to them. Father O'Leary explained all this. Then the referee called them together in the middle of the ring and talked to them.

"He's telling them that he wants a clean fight, and no punching in the clinches." Father O'Leary was the perfect guide.

The two young boxers went back to their corners and waited for the bell. When it came, one of them made the sign of the cross.

"What's he doing now?" Len enquired.

"He's making the sign of the cross."

"Will that help him?"

"Not if he can't box."

A man was playing a round of golf on an Irish golf course. It was only a social game, and the club was quite obscure. As he strolled behind his friends from the third green to the fourth tee, he saw standing beside the pathway one of the little people.

"Hey! How'd you like to hole out in one on the next hole? Think what a sensation it'd make with all your friends."

"Maybe. How much does it cost?"

"It shortens your sex life by five years."

"Okay. You're on."

On the tee he sent a strong straight drive down the fairway which bounced over the apron of the green and rolled, rolled, rolled – plop. Hole in one. Of course there was a lot of kidding about who would buy the drinks at the nineteenth hole, but eventually they played the hole out and moved on to the fifth tee.

Again our man was confronted by the leprechaun.

"Do you want to make it a double header? It's only ever been done four times in the history of golf."

"What's the damage this time?"

"Another ten years."

"Yeah. Okay."

At the fifth tee he lifted the ball with his spoon high above the water hazards. It bounced safely over the bunkers onto the green and rolled, rolled, rolled – plop. Hole in one again. This time it was on for young and old. Players were coming from all over the course with cameras and cards to be autographed. There were trunk calls to the news-

papers in Dublin. This would really put the club on the map. Finally the fuss was over, they played out the hole and moved off to the sixth tee.

Separated from the others briefly, our hero met the little green man once more.

"Why don't you bet everything you've got that you can make it three in a row? It's never been done before in the history of golf and the odds against it are astronomical."

"How much this time?"

"You can never have another thing to do with women for the rest of your life."

And that's how Father O'Flynn got his name in the Guinness Book of Records.

While Patrick was playing a round of golf with Father O'Brien, he tackled the priest about an important religious question.

"Father, do they have a golf course in heaven?"

"Well, I don't rightly know. I should think they probably have, but I don't know for sure. I'll make enquiries for you."

The following week they were having another round and Patrick raised the subject again.

"Did you find out anything about the golf courses in heaven, Father?"

"As a matter of fact I did. They've got a very fine course, and you're booked in for next Tuesday."

F ather Mulvany was fond of berating his
congregation for indulging in worldly activi-
ties like playing golf on the Sabbath. At the same
time, he was not averse to sneaking off for a quick
round himself after mass. An angel saw him one
Sunday on the seventh tee and exclaimed furiously:

"He should be punished."

God heard the angel and said:

"So he shall be. So he shall be."

Father Mulvany drove off on the 425 metre par
five hole. His ball soared down the fairway,
bounced several times and rolled along the green
till it fell gently into the cup.

The angel said to God:

"I thought you were going to punish him. You've
given him a hole in one on the longest hole on the
course."

God smiled.

"But I have punished him. Who can he tell?"

T hen there was the drunk who was playing golf with a nun. On the first tee he swung wildly.

"Dammit! I missed," he exclaimed.

The nun frowned.

Again the drunk swung, and again he missed the ball.

"Dammit! I missed again."

The nun looked stern but said nothing.

A third time the drunk swung and missed and once more let out a curse.

"Dammit! I missed."

This time Sister Josephine took him to task.

"If you continue to use this foul language, the heavens may open up and God may strike you down with a thunderbolt."

After a moment's silence the drunk addressed his ball again, swung and missed.

"DAMMIT! I missed."

The heavens were rent asunder. A lightning bolt came down and struck the nun.

A mighty voice boomed through the universe:

"DAMMIT! I MISSED."

A ttendances had fallen off at Temple so much that Rabbi Plotkin called in his two trusted friends, Maurie and Arnie.

"We have to do something I don't know what. Down the road is the Catholic church. Every Sunday morning there are so many people there you can't get a park for six blocks. What I want is that you two should go along there next Sunday and see if you can find out what the big attraction is."

Sunday morning came. Maurie and Arnie felt really strange filing into St Catherine's. But it was in a good cause and their rabbi had said it was okay. They took their places midway down the gospel side and watched closely everything that happened. Throughout the service they grew more and more excited, and as soon as mass was over could hardly wait to get back to the Temple where their rabbi was waiting for them.

"You should see the show they put on. First come out all the altar boys, cheeky little bastards, all dressed in nighties. Then comes the priest wearing a nightie all made of lace. The priest starts singing, 'I bet you I beat you at dominoes.' And all the altar boys, cheeky little bastards, they sing, 'We bet you we beat you at dominoes.' Then six fellows with baskets go round collecting the bets, and it's a sure thing for the priest every time."

T hen there was Father Birtles who, en route to Rome, found himself seated opposite a rabbi in the dining car of the train. Over a leisurely meal and a shared bottle of wine, Rabbi Mittleman and the priest became very friendly and discussed their views on many subjects, including of course their religious beliefs, laws and customs.

At length Father Birtles asked a question he'd been burning all evening to ask. In conspiratorial tones he enquired – one man of God to another: "I suppose you have done things at times which your religion denies you? I admit that I have."

"Between ourselves," replied the rabbi, "I must admit to a few misdemeanours over the years. On one occasion I ate pork which, as you know, is forbidden to us. And you? Your laws, for example, do not permit you to take to yourself a woman. Is this a law you have broken?"

"Yes," admitted Father Birtles with a faint blush. "In my young days I once did."

"Better than pork, isn't it?" grinned Mittleman.

Watching her young son busy drawing, his mother asked:
"What are you drawing, darling?"
"I'm drawing God."
"But nobody knows what God looks like."
"They will when I've finished drawing."

Father Cassidy was asking the children in the parish primary school why they believed in God.

There was a variety of answers, some full of simple faith, some obviously insincere. The one that stopped him came from young Jerome.

"I suppose it just runs in our family."

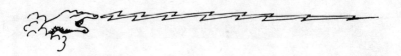

Father Gilligan was approaching the twenty-fifth anniversary of his ordination as a priest. His parishioners were wealthy and wanted to take up a collection to make him a suitable presentation. Discreet enquiries were made as to what might be a suitable gift, and Father Gilligan expressed interest in a sixteen-cylinder Cadillac. On the great day, with all the appropriate ceremony, the presentation was made.

A few days after receiving his new chariot, Father Gilligan was driving in stately fashion one hot afternoon when he came abreast of the Anglican minister trudging wearily along the side of the road. He stopped the car.

"Good afternoon, Reverend."

"Hullo, Father. My word. That's a fine-looking new car you're driving there."

"To be sure. It was a gift to me from my grateful parishioners. Would you like to come for a spin?"

"Thank you. That would be nice. I've got some time to spare."

The minister took his place in the front seat alongside Father Gilligan and they moved off. In no time they slipped through the outer suburbs into the open countryside.

"I must say it seems to handle very easily for such a big car."

"It does indeed. Would you like to take the wheel and get the feel of it?"

Suiting the actions to the words, Father Gilligan pulled the vehicle to a halt by the verge, opened the door and walked round to the passenger side.

"Slide over and have a drive."

"Oh, I couldn't really. Your lovely new car. What if anything happened?"

"Nothing's going to happen. Away you go."

The minister took the wheel very gingerly and they moved off at about twenty-five miles per hour.

"Speed it up a bit. This car can go much faster than this."

At the priest's urging the speed was gradually increased to 40 mph – 50 mph – 60 mph – 70 mph. They were doing eighty miles per hour when they hit a patch of loose gravel going round a bend. The minister lost control, and the vehicle rolled five times before it ended up against a tree.

Fortunately they were both wearing safety belts and were able to climb out. The new Cadillac was a write-off. For a time they were both so badly shaken that they couldn't speak. The minister found his voice first.

"If I wasn't a man of God, I'd swear."

"Swear and all is it?" roared Father Gilligan. "If it wasn't Ash Wednesday I'd bloody eat you."

And it was Father Gilligan again who went to a restaurant for a meal. When he ordered a bottle of wine to go with it, a nearby woman was shocked and protested. Father Gilligan calmly replied, "Do you suppose that God made all the good things of this world only for sinners?"

Some people hate to be left out of anything. A bulletin issued by the Vatican stated that there are now 143 officially recognised sins. They have received thousands of letters from all over the world asking for a copy of the complete list.

Terrence and Michael were both keen punters, but whereas Terrence always seemed to make money at it, Michael ended every race meeting losing everything he had. Finally Michael asked his friend's advice.

"What kind of a system are you using, Terry? I need something to get me out of this losing streak."

"I don't use any system at all, but I'll let you in on my secret. Opposite the main gate of the course is a little church. I always go in for a visit first and light a fifty cent candle in front of the statue of Our Lady. After that it doesn't seem to matter what I bet on, it always gets up."

Michael put this plan into operation the very next Saturday. But at the end of the day he'd lost his whole week's pay. On Monday he saw Terrence again.

"You and your bright ideas. I did everything you said and I lost a bundle."

"Can't understand it. You went into the little church across from the main gate?"

"Yes."

"And you lit a fifty cent candle in front of the statue of Our Lady?"

"Well, no. I couldn't get a fifty cent candle so I used two twenty-five cent candles."

"You silly bugger. That's the whole trouble. They're for the greyhounds."

The little old lady took her place in the confessional and, creaking in every limb, knelt to admit her transgressions. The preliminaries disposed of, she confessed that she had had sex with a man.

"When did this happen, daughter?"

"Forty-three years ago, Father."

"Then why haven't you confessed it before this?"

"Oh, I have. Several times."

"But daughter, you only need to confess a sin once. Why are you telling me again now?"

"Oh, Father. I do so like to talk about it."

"Father, I confess that I have stolen a fat chicken from someone's poultry yard," Terry whispered through the confessional screen.

"That is very wrong."

"Would you accept it, Father?"

"Certainly not. You must give it back to the man you stole it from."

"But Father, I offered it to him and he won't take it."

"In that case you may keep it yourself."

"Thank you, Father."

When the priest got home he discovered that one of his own fat chickens was missing.

St Catherine's church was undergoing alterations when Gerry went in to make his confession. When the figure appeared on the other side of the grille he said, "I've come to confess that I had sexual intercourse with three different women in the one night."

"I'm sorry. I can't help you. I'm only one of the carpenters."

"That's all right. I just had to tell someone."

Luis was confessing his sins to his parish priest.

"Father, I've sinned. I've been bedded with a married woman."

"What!" said the priest. "Carnal knowledge! God forgive such a mortal sin, and I'll need to know the name of the misbegotten sinner you slept with."

"Oh, I couldn't tell you that, Father. Where would be the honour?"

"You let me be the judge of that. Now, who was it? Was it Dolores Montez?"

"No," said Luis. "No it wasn't Dolores, Father. Don't ask me, I can't say."

"Listen, you unfortunate devil. It will go better for you if you tell who it was. Was it Carmen Fidel?"

"No, Father. It was not Mrs Fidel. Father, forgive me, but I cannot reveal who it was."

"Well, if you won't tell me, go and do penance," said the priest. "Say ten Hail Marys and three novenas."

Manuel was waiting his turn outside the confessional. "How was it? What did you get?" he whispered to Luis.

"Terrific," Luis whispered back. "Ten Hail Marys, three novenas and a couple of good leads."

Father Cassidy was in a quandary. Confession was due to start in half an hour, but he had to attend a funeral at the same time. In desperation he asked his friend Rabbi Mittleman to take his place in the confessional.

"Me? I've never done it before. What would I know from confession?"

"It's easy. Come down and I'll start you off. When you get the hang of it you can take over."

Inside the church Father Cassidy took his place in the stall with Rabbi Mittleman out of sight where he could hear what was going on. A woman entered the box.

"Father, I have sinned. I have committed adultery."

"How many times?"

"Four times, Father, and I am truly sorry."

"Say ten Hail Marys, put two dollars in the poor box, and you will be absolved."

Another woman came in.

"Father, I have sinned. I have made love to the aerobics teacher."

"How many times?"

"Twice, Father."

"Say five Hail Marys, put a dollar in the poor box, and you will be forgiven."

When she had gone, Father Cassidy whispered to Rabbi Mittleman: "See how easy it is? You can handle it. I've got to dash."

The rabbi made himself comfortable where he couldn't be seen. Another woman came in.

"What have you done, my child?" he asked.

"I have committed fornication."

"How many times?"

"Once, Father."
"Then you'd better go and do it again."
"Do it again?"
"Yes. They're on special. Two for a dollar."

A young girl went to church for confession, and said to the priest: "Oh, Father, Father, I have sinned grievously. On Monday night I slept with Sean. On Tuesday night I slept with Patrick, and on Wednesday night I slept with Mick. Oh Father, Father, what shall I do?"

"My child, my child," replied the priest, "go home and squeeze the juice from a whole lemon and drink it."

"Oh Father, Father, will this purge me of my sin?" she asked.

"No child, but it will wipe the smile off your face."

A young couple rushed into Father Cassidy's study and stammered out their request.

"We want to get married as soon as possible. We've got all the papers. You'll find they're in order. Your housekeeper and gardener will do as witnesses."

Father Cassidy smiled and performed the ceremony. But as he gratefully pocketed a fifty dollar bill he said: "You know the old saying about marrying in haste. What's the hurry?"

Halfway out the door the young man made his reply.

"We're double parked."

T he bride was a vision in white, her hair bedecked with lace and orange blossom. The groom, in full morning dress, stood tall and handsome. Only the quivering of elegant grey gloves clasped in his left hand betrayed his emotions.

They were standing before the altar to be married when the bride suddenly whispered to the priest:

"Father, you're reading the burial service."

"Sure now," the priest whispered back, "it doesn't matter. You'll be under the sod tonight either way."

"Do you take this man to be your lawful wedded husband, for better or for worse?"

"Just as he is, Father. Just as he is. If he gets any better the good Lord will take him, and if he gets any worse, I'll attend to him myself."

Then there was the wedding service conducted by Father Cassidy. At the appointed time he turned to the young woman in white before him and solemnly enquired: "Do you promise to obey this man for as long as you shall live?"

The bride was indignant.

"Do you think I'm crazy?"

The nervous groom thought it was his cue.

"I do," he said.

A man who had been married twelve months earlier met the officiating priest for the first time since the ceremony.

"Listen, Father. You told me when you married us that I was at the end of my troubles."

"So I did," said the priest, "but I didn't say which end."

In some of the South American countries it is quite common for parents to name a boy Jesus. There was one such boy in the choir of San Salvator's. He had a really angelic appearance, but a harsh and untuneful voice. The parish priest used to let him stand in the front of the choir where he looked the part beautifully. He did not sing, but mouthed the words to give the appearance of singing.

Jesus was in the forefront of the choir when the Bishop came for his annual visit to San Salvator's. After mass was said, His Grace tackled the parish priest about the boy's performance.

"You know that little dark boy in the front of the choir? He wasn't singing at all. He was just opening and closing his mouth."

"Oh, Jesus. He can't sing."

"No, but Christ he could try, couldn't he?"

Terry and Clancy were fishing on Sunday morning, and Terry was feeling very guilty about it.

"I suppose we should have gone to mass," he said.

Clancy was unconcerned.

"I couldn't have gone anyway. The wife's sick in bed."

"I didn't see you in church last Sunday. I heard you were playing golf."

"That's not true, Father. I've got the fish to prove it."

B illy Graham was conducting a crusade in Ireland. Late one afternoon he went walking along the clifftops. After a time he came upon two Protestants pulling a Catholic up the cliff out of the sea by a rope.

"This is a fine act of Christian charity you are doing," he exclaimed. "The Lord will bless you for it." And he strode off along the cliff path with an uplifted heart.

"Who was that?" said one of the Protestants as soon as Graham was out of sight.

"That was Dr Billy Graham. He knows more about the Bible than any other man in the world."

"Perhaps so, but he doesn't know much about shark fishing."

F ather Cassidy had a real passion for football, and whenever he could persuade his curate to take confession he would be off on Saturday afternoon to watch his favourite team. He hadn't missed a grand final in years and this year was no exception. There he was in the grandstand, dressed, as always on these occasions, in plain clothes, so that he could feel like one of the boys.

At half time he fancied a pint, but when he got to the bar the crowd was six deep. He was about to give up hope when a friendly man in a priestly dog collar offered to buy a pint for him. As the good Samaritan approached the bar, the crowd parted for him like the Red Sea before Moses and he returned moments later with brimming glasses.

"Thank you," Father Cassidy said. "As a matter of fact I'm a priest myself. I just put on ordinary clothes for the footy so as to be one of the boys."

"Funny you should say that," the stranger replied. "I'm not a priest at all myself. But in this gear I can always get through to the bar at half time."

There was a great to-do, fanned by most of the newspapers in the land, when a priest declined to read the burial service over a former member of the Masonic Lodge.

Terry asked his own priest:

"Father, would you refuse to bury a Mason?"

"Refuse? Not at all. I only wish I could be burying them all day long."

A Catholic family and a Protestant family shared a holiday house at the coast. The weather was warm and the beach secluded so the parents let the little Catholic boy and Protestant girl, both aged five, swim without any costumes. When they came out of the water they were asked:

"Did you enjoy your swim?"

"Yes we did, thank you. And not only that. Now we know what the difference is between a Catholic and a Protestant."

After cigars and port, the squire took his son Chudleigh into the library.

"My boy," he began, "it's time for us to have a little talk. You're twenty-five years of age. You know the facts of life. You've been to Eton and Cambridge. You've knocked about for a few years. Now it's time you thought about settling down and getting married.

"When I die, all these estates, all my interests in the city will pass on to you, and I would like to know that you in turn had someone to pass them on to.

"Now, take the Lady Muriel. She's a healthy sort. Plays a good stick of tennis and golf. Not a bad seat on a horse. She'd be a good breeder. Why don't you marry the Lady Muriel?"

"But Father, I don't love the Lady Muriel."

"Oh, love is it? Well what about the Lady Cynthia? She's a nice little piece of goods. A charming hostess and a pretty dancer. Just the sort of girl to smooth away the worries after a hard day in the city. Why don't you marry the Lady Cynthia?"

"But Father, I don't love the Lady Cynthia."

"Well damn it all, who do you love?"

"Well Father, I am rather keen on Lord Lonsdale."

"Lord Lonsdale? You can't marry him. He's a Catholic!"

In the early days of heart transplants a successful operation was performed on Whispering Willie, the international con man. As soon as he was discharged from hospital Willie flew to Rome and set up an audience with His Holiness the Pope. With an air of great secrecy he whispered his story. For some time during his operation he had been clinically dead. He'd been to the hereafter. There was no-one there. All he asked to keep this a secret was five million US dollars.

His Holiness was distraught. If a story like this should spread it could undermine the faith of millions all around the world. He consulted with his advisers and somehow the money was found.

Not satisfied with this coup, Willie flew on to Moscow where he had a discussion with the heads of the Kremlin. He had been dead. He had seen Him. He was there all right. All their efforts to persuade the masses that religion was a lot of hogwash would go down the tube if he told his story. All he wanted to keep it quiet was five million US dollars. The Russians pondered a short time, then paid.

One more move and Willie's game would be complete. He flew to Washington DC. But Willie never made it to the White House. The minute he walked down the gangway of the jet he was surrounded by secret service men.

"We know what you're up to, Willie. We heard all about your little tricks in Rome and Moscow. You needn't think you're going to get any easy money here."

"Not even if I say that He's black?"

Father Whelan had become so tired and run down that his doctor feared that he would go into depression. Accordingly he arranged a consultation for the priest with a psychiatrist. After a preliminary interview the specialist gave Father Whelan some serious advice.

"You've got into this state because you've gone for so long without a holiday. Nobody's indispensable, Father, not even you. Now what I want you to do is have a real holiday. Get some ordinary clothes and head off to Paris for a few weeks. Forget all about your parish. Forget that you're even a priest. Just relax, take it easy and be one of the boys."

Father Whelan made arrangements for another priest to look after his parish, dressed himself in plain clothes and headed for Paris. He spent the first ten days doing the things that all tourists do, and then decided he'd like to go to a sex show. Without his clerical garb nothing could be simpler. He paid his money and in he went.

A number of attractive young women with very few clothes danced on the small stage and down among the tables. One particularly nice little girl danced near his table, and he was just reaching out to pinch her on the bottom when she seized his wrist.

"No you don't, Father."

"How did you know I was a priest?"

"Because I'm Sister Theresa. I go to the same psychiatrist that you do."

"Drink," thundered the priest, "is the greatest curse of mankind. It makes you quarrel with your neighbours. It makes you spend all your rent money. It makes you shoot at your landlord – and it makes you miss him!"

On another occasion, that same reverend thunderer was treating his flock to a grand old-fashioned "hell-fire" sermon, repeating at frequent intervals the phrase, "There shall be weeping and gnashing of teeth".

Exasperated by this repetition, an aged member of the congregation shouted, "Let 'em gnash 'em as 'as 'em."

To which the priest rejoined, "Madam, teeth will be provided."

Three drunks were in a bar during one of Pope Pius's illnesses. An argument sprang up between two of them.

"I know who the next Pope will be. It'll be Cardinal Spellman."

"Rubbish. The next Pope will be Cardinal Gilroy."

"He couldn't win with a start. It'll be Cardinal Spellman."

"Cardinal Gilroy."

"Cardinal Spellman."

The third drunk had said nothing up to now. He interrupted the other two.

"Neither of you blokes knows what he's talking about. I know who the next Pope'll be."

"All right. Who is it?"

"The Archbishop of Canterbury."

"Don't be stupid. He's not even a Catholic."

"Oh well, if you're going to drag religion into it I won't even argue with you."

F ather Cassidy was becoming very concerned about the amount of heavy drinking among the men of the parish. He preached a sermon in which he told the story of a Mexican peasant who worked all through the heat of the morning with his donkey. When he broke off at midday he gave the donkey a bucket of beer to drink. The donkey tasted it, but would not drink. Then the peasant gave the donkey a bucket of water and the donkey drank every drop.

"Why was it that the donkey drank the water, but would not drink the beer?" Father Cassidy demanded of the congregation.

A voice from the back of the church supplied the answer.

"Because he was a donkey, that's why."

"T errence, why is it that every Sunday as soon as you leave the church you head straight into the Plough Inn?"

"Well, Father, I suppose that's what you'd call a 'thirst after righteousness'."

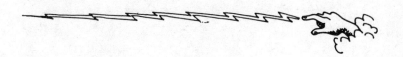

Then there was old Paddy who was caught trying to smuggle a jar of whiskey across the border from Eire to Northern Ireland.

"What's in the jar?"

"Holy water."

The inspector opened it and sniffed.

"Good God, man. This is whiskey."

"Saints be praised. It's a miracle."

On a long train journey Father Fitzgerald took along his Bible to read, but the only other occupant of the compartment was a drunk who wanted to talk.

"What's the book you're reading, your reverence?"

"This is the Bible that I'm trying to read," sighed the priest.

"The Bible, eh? What's it about?"

"Haven't you ever read the Bible? What a pity. The Bible is a veritable treasure house of stories, poetry and teaching handed down to us from the ancients." By now well into his subject, Father Fitzgerald continued with passion: "Why right now I'm reading a fascinating story about Samson. In his day he was the strongest man in the world. One day when he was in the fields there came over the hill five thousand Philistines. Samson took the jawbone of an ass and slew five hundred of them and routed the rest."

The drunk was very impressed by all this. That evening he told his mate about it over a few pints.

"I'm going to get a Bible."

"No kidding. What for?"

"Well, on the train I got talking to this priest and he was telling me about all these beaut adventure stories that are in it. Like there's this bloke Simpson who was a real tough. One day he's out in the fields, see, and who comes over the hill but fifty thousand Filipinos. But Simpson attacked them with just the arse bone of a Jew. He killed five thousand of them, and I'd hate to tell you what he did to the rest of 'em."

On another train journey two labourers were arguing whether a certain peculiarly dressed passenger was the Archbishop of Westminster. In the end they had a small bet about it. One of them approached the gentleman and enquired politely:

"Pardon me, Guv, but are you the Archbishop of Westminster?"

"What the bleedin' hell has that got to do with you?" was the reply.

The workman returned to his mate and reported.

"It's no use. The old goat won't give a straight answer one way or the other."

The Bishop was visiting a psychiatric hospital where he was introduced to a patient who said he was God.

"I'm honoured to meet you," he said. "I believe you are God."

"I am."

"Good. There's a little question I'd like to ask you about making the world in six days. Isn't that a figure of speech? Shouldn't it be six centuries or ages?"

The patient addressed him gravely, "Your Grace, I make it a rule never to talk shop."

It was a cold night, pouring with rain. An old man fell dying into the gutter. A bystander rushed up to help.

"What can I do? Where do you live? What's your name?" he asked.

"I'm Sean O'Reilly. There's nothing you can do. I'm dying."

"Shall I fetch Father Cassidy?"

"No. Fetch Rabbi Plotkin."

"Are you sure? With a name like Sean O'Reilly you want the rabbi and not the priest?"

"To be sure. I wouldn't think of dragging Father Cassidy out on a night like tonight."

Then there was Clancy on his deathbed. The priest in attendance asked him if he renounced the devil.

"I don't know, Father," replied Clancy. "I'm thinking it might not be a good time for making enemies."

Old Mary O'Connor, noted for her bad temper, finally died. After the requiem mass, her coffin was lowered into the grave and the earth was shovelled in. Just when the job was complete, a tremendous clap of thunder sounded overhead.

Her husband looked up.

"Sounds as if she made it," he said.

Twelve wives arrived in purgatory. The angel in charge came forward to receive them and take their particulars.

"Now then ladies, how many of you have been unfaithful to your husbands?" he asked.

Eleven of them shyly raised their hands. The angel sighed and picked up the phone.

"Is that hell? Have you got room for twelve unfaithful wives – one of them stone deaf?"

S t Peter was interviewing a new arrival at the pearly gates.

"What's your name?"

"Irving."

"When you were on earth did you ever drink or smoke or gamble?"

"No sir."

"Did you ever lie or cheat or steal or swear?"

"No sir, I did not."

"Were you promiscuous?"

"No, I was not."

"Tell me – what took you so long?"

O ld Bridget's pet cat died, so she went to Father Gilligan to arrange for his funeral.

"Am I to understand that you want me to bury a cat in the graveyard? Certainly not."

"Then I can't give you the $10,000 he left the Church in his will."

"Oh! Why didn't you tell me he was a Catholic cat?"

A famous surgeon died and went to heaven. The angel at the pearly gates asked him:

"Is there anything on your mind you'd like to tell me about before you come in?"

"Yes there is. When I was a junior surgeon at St Bartholomew's I played for the hospital football team. We had one close-fought match against Guy's in which I scored a goal. I thought it was offside, but the referee allowed it and we went on to win the match."

"That's perfectly all right. We know all about that little incident and you needn't worry at all."

"Thank you very much St Peter. I feel much better about it now."

"Oh, I'm not St Peter," said the angel. "I'm St Bartholomew."

A bridge had been washed away and a trainload of 723 pilgrims on its way to Lourdes plunged into a ravine. There were no survivors.

Presently the unfortunate victims found themselves outside the pearly gates where St Peter was on duty – the eternal-day shift. The pilgrims elected a spokesman and he approached the venerable presence.

"Who are you lot?" roared the saint, disconcerted by the milling crowd.

"We're 723 Catholic pilgrims. We were on our way to Lourdes when we were all killed in a train smash. Can we come in?"

St Peter became instantly sympathetic.

"Well, normally I'd have no hesitation in letting you in, but right now we're really strapped for accommodation. There's been a flood in China, earthquakes in Mexico and a long drought in Africa. We're full to bursting. The new places won't be ready for another two weeks."

"What are we going to do? We can't stay out here for two weeks."

"I'll have to see if I can fix you up with some alter-native accommodation."

He picked up a phone.

"Nick? Pete here. We've got a bit of a problem. I'm hoping you can help us out. There's this bunch of 723 Catholics want to come in and we've got nowhere to put them. Can you find somewhere for them for a couple of weeks?"

"Catholics? You're asking a lot, aren't you? Oh well, I suppose it'll be okay as long as it's not more than two weeks."

St Peter turned to the spokesman.

"Just step into the lift and press the Down button."

A week later, Nick was on the phone talking desperately to Pete.

"Pete. You've got to get those Catholics out of here right now. What with their baccarat schools and their bingo, they're only $200 short of airconditioning the place."

The operation, as they say, was a success but the patient died, and soon thereafter he was fronting the pearly gates through which St Peter ushered him. He was then passed on to St Michael for an orientation tour. First to the robing chambers for a tailor-made kaftan, thence to brassware for halo and harp. Thus equipped, the newcomer stood with St Michael before the expanse of paradise.

"I'll just explain the layout to you," St Michael gestured as they walked along. "Over there by the river you'll find the Presbyterians. The Methodists like to congregate down in that bottom field. The Anglicans usually gather in those pastures green over there and the Baptists in that forest yonder."

St Michael was in the middle of a directory to the stamping grounds of assorted American schisms when they approached a five-metre-high brick wall.

"Ssh," hissed the sainted one. "We'll have to tiptoe past this."

The newcomer raised a questioning eyebrow.

"It's the Catholics you see. They think they're the only ones up here."